WHAT HAVE WE BECOME?

Where Are We Going?

PERNELL STONEY

Copyright © 2016 by Pernell Stoney

What Have We Become?
Where Are We Going?
by Pernell Stoney

Printed in the United States of America.

ISBN 9781498473903

All rights reserved solely by the author. The author guarantees all contents are original and do not infringe upon the legal rights of any other person or work. No part of this book may be reproduced in any form without the permission of the author. The views expressed in this book are not necessarily those of the publisher.

Scripture quotations taken from the King James Version (KJV)
– *public domain*

www.xulonpress.com

Contents

Introduction vii
Acknowledgments xi
Dedication xv

Chapter 1: The Antichrist Is Here! 17
Chapter 2: Disobedience 25
Chapter 3: Man vs. God 37
Chapter 4: What You Can Do 53
Chapter 5: Prayer, Praise, and
           Thanksgiving 69
Chapter 6: The End-Time Is Near—
           Are You Spiritually
           Ready? 85
Chapter 7: The Promises of God 107

Introduction

Today, men and women—believers and unbelievers alike—lack the knowledge of what they are saying and doing, and the effect it has on their and others' lives. Tragically, this lack of knowledge is taught daily on television shows, at the movies, in the streets, at home, in the media, and, yes, in some churches. We are teaching our sons and daughters in a way contrary to what the Bible tells us, even the use of negative language. This way of life comes from a lack of understanding that the things we say and do can really affect people. The bottom line: Satan has deafened our ears to what God's Word has told us to do.

However, if we, as God's people—we are *all* God's people; we just have to accept Him)—would study His Word, we would come to know that the things we say and do determine who we will become. Currently, our lifestyles are far from honoring God. As men and women of God, we need to renew our thought patterns through the Word of God. Then, His Word will teach us the ingredients we need to honor Him and act and speak positively.

Until then, our children will continue to be lost because they don't see the Spirit of God in their parents or their friends. All of us, while here in the flesh, need to get filled with the Spirit of God.

This book will present you with Scriptures from the Old and New

Introduction

Testaments that will prove to you that God wants you to be positive. It also shows the importance of your actions based on speaking and developing a relationship with Him and loving one another. As you read my eye-opening, life-changing experience, I hope it will change you the way it has changed me. I pray to God that you will hear what He is saying to you and be able to experience the great joy of being open and obedient to our Lord and Savior, Jesus Christ. After all, God did not make a mistake, and you are just who you were when you were born.

Acknowledgments

First, I give thanks and honor to my Lord and Savior, Jesus Christ, for it is through His blood that I am saved; to my wife, Hwason, a true friend and woman of God, for still loving me after thirty-six years of bad and good times; to my daughter, Cherry, one of the sweetest people you could ever meet, who is always thinking of others first; and to my son, Steven, a man with strong family values, who is always in my heart with a love that is unmatched.

In addition, I would like to thank my spiritual families: Minister Johnny, Robin and Moses Williams, Pastor James, and GiGi and DD Williams. We love you with the love of God. God has given all of you a heart of love and care; thank you for being there for us.

Thanks go to Dr. Michael and Brineta Mitchell, my mentor and longtime friends of Restoration Ministries International (RMI) Christian Fellowship in Augusta, Georgia, for teaching us the Word of God. To Dr. Ron and Sue Rockwell, our pastors and spiritual leaders at Harvest Church in Phoenix, Arizona, thanks for being an example of not only teaching, but living a spiritual life the past seven years. Thanks for teaching us how to love one another the way God wants us to. Special thanks go to apostle John Evans for letting me know it was not my fault, but it was my time.

Also, special thanks go to my new pastors, Mirek and Linda Hufton of World

Acknowledgments

Harvest Church in Roswell, Georgia, who boldly teach the Word of God, letting us know how to be strong and bold in the Word of God.

Again, thanks to all our friends. Remember, God loves you, and so do we.

Dedication

This book is dedicated to all people in hopes that they will return to their first love and follow His commandment to love one another as they love themselves—with a giving love that fills them up each day with joy and happiness, respecting and thinking of others, being willing to sacrifice for their neighbors, to let them know the time is near and we must be ready. Remember, "Be not afraid, only believe" (Mark 5:36).

Chapter 1

The Antichrist Is Here!

I ask, "What have we become?" to get you thinking about the things we are doing that are against the Word of God. I believe we have been blinded by the work of the devil. If you don't know whose you are, you will follow anyone. We have been given a bull to ride, and it has gotten out of control. We have allowed the media, political agendas, and man as a whole to be influenced by the wicked ways of the devil to create confusion among God's people. From my view, we are headed straight to hell.

While we are not perfect people, we serve a perfect God, and He has left instructions for us to follow, if we trust and believe in Him and His Word. However, we, as Christians, have become weak in our faith and trust in God. But beware! When you become weak, the enemy will attack and overrun you. This is exactly what we have allowed to happen to us—we're allowing the work of the devil to call bad things good and good things bad (Isaiah 5:20). For example, there is an NFL player who comes on the field with Bible verses on his eyelids (including Philippians 4:13, which says, "I can do all things through Christ which strengtheneth me"). He was ridiculed for doing that, along with going to one knee and giving God thanks. On the flip side, another NFL player stated he was gay, and everyone praised him for saying so; the NFL even made special rules for him so he would be accepted. I agree, we should accept him as a man that God created and love him for that reason alone, but we should not put him on top of the world for others to admire.

This direction we are going in did not just start last week, last year, or even five years ago. Rather, it started a very long time ago. If you would read God's Word, you would know what is happening. I am going to write what it tells us, in case you don't read the Bible yourself. Let's start at the beginning, in the book of Genesis. You can read all of it, but chapter 2 talks about the creation of man, and chapter 6 talks about the fall of man. I want you to read the Bible to confirm what I am telling you (King James Version). When you read the Word, please read it with an open mind; look around you and see what is happening. This also will confirm what the Word of God is saying and has been saying for the past two thousand years.

Please don't get this wrong. We are to love *everyone,* even those who claim to be female who were born male and those who were born female and claim to be male. According to the Word of God, we are to love them, but we don't have to accept or love *what they are doing.* Because God does not make mistakes, who you were when you were born—male or female—is who you are in God's eyes. Putting on a dress does not make you a woman, just as putting on a pair of slacks does not make you a man. The biggest sports awards show gave an award for courage to a man who changed his God-given body from male to female. Personally, I don't want the type of courage that goes against what God the Father created us to be. This is the type of action that brought death and separation from the Father.

My question is, who is this award lifting up? It's not lifting up God. Men and women are accepting things like this, which go against the Word of God. Furthermore, the Supreme Court went from being men and women to playing God by making same-sex marriage legal. When man puts himself above God, changing what the Creator has created, that is an open door to big trouble. If you don't know the order of things, go back to the beginning, to the One who created those things; that is the only way to get it right. If He said to be fruitful and multiply, please tell me how this will happen if two men or two women get married. This is not in God's plan for mankind. (Read Genesis chapter 1; see especially verse 28). When man begins to change the laws of God, we, as believers of God, allow things like that to happen. We are at as much fault as they are.

God has given us power to overcome things like that. His Word says, "Greater is he that is in us than he that is in the world." Jesus told the disciples that the Father would send another comforter; He's referring to the Holy Spirit.

The plan and action you are witnessing today is the plan of the Antichrist, and people are falling right into his plan, believing that things that are happening are right and good. Even the media is falling into the devil's plan; everywhere you look, things that are bad are being called good, and things that are good are called bad. Men, women, and children are being healed, miracles are taking place daily, and people still don't believe or have faith in God. The book of Hosea 4:6 says: "My people are destroyed for lack of knowledge: because thou hast rejected knowledge, I will also reject thee, that thou shalt be no priest to me: seeing thou hast forgotten the law of thy God, I will also forget thy children." All you have to do is look around and see that His Word is true. The Antichrist is here, and he is leading people to hell!

Chapter 2

Disobedience

To learn more about why this is happening today, we can turn to the book of Romans chapters 1 and 2.

Reasons for Guilt

To learn the reasons for our guilt, read the following verses from Romans chapter 1.

Verse 18: "For the wrath of God is revealed from heaven against all ungodliness and unrighteousness of men, who hold the truth in unrighteousness."

Verses 19-21: "Because that which may be known of God is manifest in them; for God hath shewed it unto them. For the invisible things of him from the creation of the world are clearly seen, being understood by the things that are made, even his eternal power and Godhead; so that they are without excuse: Because that, when they knew God, they glorified him not as God, neither were thankful; but became vain in their imaginations, and their foolish heart was darkened" (the Supreme Court members).

Verses 22-23: "Professing themselves to be wise, they became fools, and changed the glory of the uncorruptible God into an image made like to corruptible man, and to birds, and fourfooted beasts, and creeping things."

Results of Guilt

To learn the results of that guilt, read these verses from the same chapter in Romans:

Verse 24: "Wherefore God also gave them up to uncleanness through the lusts of their own hearts, to dishonour their own bodies between themselves . . . ."

Verse 25: "Who changed the truth of God into a lie, and worshipped and served the creature more than the Creator, who is blessed forever. Amen."

Verse 26: "For this cause God gave them up unto vile affections: for even their women did change the natural use into that which is against nature . . . ."

Verses 27-32: "And likewise also the men, leaving the natural use of the woman, burned in their lust one toward another; men with men working that which is unseemly, and receiving in themselves that recompence of their error which was meet. And even as they did not like to retain God in their knowledge, God gave them over to a reprobate mind, to do those things which are not convenient; being filled with all unrighteousness, fornication, wickedness, covetousness, maliciousness; full of envy, murder, debate, deceit, malignity; whisperers, backbiters, haters of God, despiteful, proud, boasters, inventors of evil things, disobedient to parents, without understanding, covenantbreakers, without natural affection, implacable, unmerciful: who knowing the judgment of God, that they which commit such things are worthy of death, not only do the same, but have pleasure in them that do them."

The Word of God spells it out for us; all we need to do is read His Word and apply it to our lives. First, we must understand we are in a spiritual war, and that war is being fought in the spirit realm. The fight is over controlling our minds. If Satan is controlling our minds, he knows our flesh comes with our minds. The Antichrist is already here and taking over the minds of young and old alike. Look around, and see what is going on. We are losing this fight!

However, if you are a true believer in the Father, Son, and Holy Spirit, you have the victory! You just need to get into a boot camp (a Bible study or church) to learn how to defend yourself against the enemy, for the Word of God tells us, "GREATER is he that is in you, than he that is in the world" (1 John 4:4, emphasis added). To explain what this means, he that is in us—the Spirit of God—is greater than he that is in the world—the devil, or the prince of this world, whose mission is to destroy the lives of nonbelievers by trying to stop them from trusting and believing in our Lord and Savior, Jesus Christ. If your spirit life is weak, you will be overtaken by the wickedness of this world.

If we don't have a strong foundation built on the Father, Son, and Holy Spirit, we are prime targets to be recruited by Satan's army. When this happens, we are brought into a world of sin, living as modern-day Sodoms and Gomorrahs. My questions are, What have we done? And where are we going? I will answer these with what I believe the Holy Spirit has revealed to me, and I'm sure I am not the only one to whom the Holy Spirit has revealed this. We have defiled the living God with disobedient thinking. We are God's children, and we can change what we want and don't have to answer to anyone. We don't know whom we are fighting against; the devil has caused division among us, and a house divided cannot stand (Mark 3:25). As this division is occurring, we lack the knowledge of what is going on. Hosea 4:6 tells us: "My people are destroyed for lack of knowledge: because thou hast rejected knowledge, I will also reject thee, that thou shalt be no priest to me: seeing thou hast forgotten the law of thy God, I will also forget thy children."

If you look around, you will see this is already happening daily. We have five judges who think they are gods, changing what the Creator has set in motion, making up laws as they go. If we don't stop and repent, we will be on our way to hell in a handbasket. If you don't know, hell *is* a real place. As Psalm 9:17 states, "The wicked shall be turned into hell, and all the nations that forget God." And according to Proverbs 27:20, "Hell and destruction are never full; so the eyes of man are never satisfied."

Living by the principles and guidelines that the Creator has set is not enough for man. We have to change things, creating confusion for the weak, leading them straight to hell. Also, I believe, the spiritual leaders of this world have grown weak. Because we have become weak, fearing man more than God, the true standard of righteous living is slipping away.

Of many examples I can use, I want to use this one: A man who owned a bakery refused to bake a cake for two men getting married. They sued him, and the courts tried to force him to do what he believes is wrong. By baking the cake, he felt he would've been taking part in something the Bible says is sin. He is correct. You can read about this yourself in the book of Romans. That is just the tip of the explosion that is about to come.

Furthermore, parents have gotten weak and are letting their children do what they want, wear what they want, and say what they want. Some say, "It's just kids being kids; it's all part of growing up." Well, let me tell you something: Look around at what is happening. Our children are being killed because we are not teaching them. However, we, as Christians, have a duty and responsibility to teach our children because God has told us: "And thou shalt teach them diligently unto thy children, and shalt talk of them when thou sittest in thine house, and when thou walkest by the way, and when thou liest down, and when thou risest up" (Deuteronomy 6:7). But we can't do that because we have let social media take our place as parents. We don't even spend time with one another because we are all doing our own thing on the phone, Facebook, Instagram, Snapchat, or another distraction that is keeping us from teaching our children the Word of God. If we don't teach them, the world will, and you can see what they are learning is not good.

We are in a spiritual battle, which started with our leaders and is working its way down. Not all, but many pastors are jealous of other pastors and are putting them down in front of the world. Stealing other church members, being blinded by the devil, and forgetting that the people don't belong to them, but to God, are a few things we're seeing at churches. They are seeing who can build the biggest church, not realizing it is not the size of the church that will get them or their followers into heaven. It is time to get back to the *basic instruction before leaving earth* (BIBLE). How will we do that? I'm glad you asked . . . .

Chapter 3

Man vs. God

We have allowed the cunningness of Satan to deceive us, just like he did Eve in the garden. (Please read Genesis 3:1-6.) We fear man more than God, and that can't be good for the people who are not saved. Politics are not above God, yet we who are saved are going along with the sinful decisions that are being made, doing what I call "sin support." Remember, we can still love the individuals who are sinning without loving, or even liking, what they are doing. We must pray for them and let God deal with them. We are under a higher power than man. We are to respect man and not be afraid of him. After all, the Word tells us, "If God be for us, who can be against us?" (Romans 8:31). When we accept the Word of God with a trusting heart and a believing attitude, we will accept what it says in His Word. (Read Romans 8:30-39.)

When man goes against God, he will lose every time. I don't know about you, but I like to be on the winning side. The Word of God tells us we all will suffer persecution, and there will be trials and tribulations. The question is can you, will you, stand? And when you can't stand, will you trust in the Lord and not man? Don't feel alone, embarrassed, or left out because you are not alone in going the way of the world. Remember, the Word tells us, "Greater is he that is in you, than he that is in the world" (1 John 4:4). Therefore, we have to make the necessary adjustments to get back on track with the Word of God. We must know we have the victory in Christ Jesus, so why are we caving in the ways of the world? When we stand up for God, He will fight our battles.

The fivefold ministry needs to stand up together as a unit on the Word of God and be bold, letting the world know we are children of the most high God and we will be obedient to His Word. One thing we must do, and that is let go of our personal feelings and let the Holy Spirit do what He was sent to do: lead us into all truths. We must stop leaning on our own understanding, which has weakened us in the things of the Lord, causing us to go along with the things of the world—against the will of God. All I am asking you to do is read God's Word with an open mind, asking Him to give you the understanding you need to make the correct decision.

I was once where you are, full of doubt and unbelief. But having a praying and praising grandmother got me through, as did getting married to my gift from God, whom God changed to a praying wife, which in turn changed me into a praying man and husband. I give God thanks every day for what He has done for me! Though I had to take the first step, once I did, He began to work on me. God has given all of us free will; He will not force us to do anything. It is we who make the choice to take a chance and change (the three C's of life).

We can't be on the side of man, but instead need to heed the Word of God. His Word tells us if we deny Him before man, He will deny us before the Father:

"But whosoever shall deny me before men, him will I also deny before my Father which is in heaven" (Matthew 10:33). Sitting around not doing or saying anything makes us just as guilty. Those of us who have the platform to speak out should, as being silent is not the way of Christ followers. As I said before, while we are to love *everyone,* we don't have to like what others are doing. We still must pray for them and let God do what He will do. The bottom line: We can't fight against God and expect to win. I am sure He will have the last word.

We are headed the wrong way. When we think we are more powerful than God, the Creator, we have a big problem. We cannot change what God has put in motion; we are not authorized to mess with His creation. Therefore, when we do that without His permission, we will feel His anger.

What Have We Become?

The following are twelve excuses for not following God's Word that man has made you believe. While there are many more, I wanted to bring these to your attention. The first excuse is a sugarcoated term for "fear" that the devil is using to keep you from what the Word of God tells us. Remember what the Word says about fear: "For God hath not given us the spirit of fear; but of power, and of love, and of a sound mind" (2 Timothy 1:7). Don't ever forget this!

These excuses are not in any particular order, as each person acts differently according to his or her priorities. The bottom line is these excuses have touched all of us at some point in our walk to Jesus, or not.

On some of these, you will have to fill in the blank. This is just to get you to read the Bible and know what it says.

Excuse: "I am not a sinner."
Answer: "For all have _sinned_, and come short of the glory of God" (Romans 3:23). My question to you: If you are not a sinner, are you keeping God's Word, and are you applying Matthew 22:37?

Excuse: "My family members are not believers."
Answer: Being a believer is not a group thing. Of course, we all want our family to be saved. But being saved and having God be the head of your life is a personal decision and done individually.

Excuse: "I am not as good as others."
Answer: We need to live by standards and not by comparisons. "For we dare not . . . compare ourselves with some that commend themselves: but they measuring themselves by themselves,

and comparing themselves among themselves, are not wise" (2 Corinthians 10:12). This is where we get in trouble, trying to be like someone else whom God did not intend for us to be. Instead, measure yourself by Jesus if you want to know how good or bad you are. Remember, you are not lost or saved by the deeds of others.

Excuse: "I don't feel anything."
Answer: The Word of God doesn't operate by feelings; it operates on FAITH (forward action in trust in Him/forsaking all, I trust Him). Most people do most of their worthy acts contrary to feeling. For example, a doctor does not deal with sickness or diseases because of their feelings, but because of necessity. Acting on feelings gets us in a lot of trouble. You may say, "I feel like a woman," or "I feel like a man." Because you feel that way

does not give you the right to change what God has created!

Excuse: "I am weak."
Answer: "Thou wilt keep him in perfect peace, whose mind is stayed on thee: because he trusteth in thee. Trust ye in the Lord for ever: for in the Lord Jehovah is everlasting _strength_" (Isaiah 26:3-4). Who will keep you? The _Lord_ God. How? "In _perfect peace_." Whom will He keep? Those "whose _mind is_" on God and not on self or circumstances or others. What we need to do is trust and not worry. You may be asking, "Trust in whom?" Trust in God. "How long?" Always—He has everlasting strength.

Excuse: "I am doing the best I can."
Answer: How long have you been doing your best? Have you succeeded? How

long will it take to make yourself ready for heaven? What if you die today? The number one thing you can do is believe. You cannot do anything to save yourself except have faith, trust, and belief in God. That is doing your best!

Excuse: "There are too many hypocrites."

Answer: Please understand this: Hypocrites are lost people. If you let hypocrites keep you from being saved, you could spend eternity in hell with them. When you hide behind something, you are smaller than what you are hiding behind. So if you are hiding behind a hypocrite, you are smaller than that person. (Read Acts 17:30-31, Romans 14:12, and Matthew 7:1-5.) My brothers and sisters, don't let man suck you into his rebellious, changing laws. God does not like what He sees, and a price will need to be paid for what is happening. So please don't get caught up in this modern-day Sodom and Gomorrah.

Excuse: "I do not understand."
Answer: Why let mystery cause you to refuse the Savior? Do you understand how your digestive system works? Does your ignorance of it keep you from eating pizza, steak, or any other type of food? Do you understand why the sun rises in the East and sets in the West? Do you understand why the same sun is hotter in Arizona than in Georgia? Lay aside your excuse of not understanding, and trust God as you trust your cell phone to post things on Facebook or Instagram (Romans 11:33 and 2 Corinthians 2:14).

Excuse: "People will laugh at me."

Answer: It is better that *they* laugh than God. "I also will laugh at your calamity; I will mock when your fear cometh" (Proverbs 1:26). Shun evil companions. "Enter not into the path of the wicked, and go not in the way of evil men. . . . The way of the wicked is as darkness: they know not at what they stumble" (Proverbs 4:14, 19). Do not be ashamed of Christ. Matthew 10:32-33 adds: "Whosoever therefore shall confess me before men, him will I confess also before my Father which is in heaven. But whosoever shall deny me before men, him will I also deny before my Father which is in heaven."

Excuse: "I am going to have a good time in this world and let the next world take care of itself."

Answer: Many have followed this way of thinking and living. But Luke 16:25 tells us, "Son, remember that thou in thy lifetime receivedst thy good things, and likewise Lazarus evil things: but now he is comforted, and thou art tormented." Your life can prove to be a charade (Luke 12:15). Remember, opportunity brings responsibility (Ecclesiastes 11:9). When we look at things in the past and now, there are always people who take the wide road of destruction with lights and glitter, their eyes blinded by the things this world has to offer, not knowing there are greater rewards in heaven for those who accept Jesus as their Lord and Savior. Matthew 16:26 reminds us of this: "For what is a man profited, if he shall gain the whole world, and lose his own soul?"

Excuse: "I am my own boss; no one tells me what to do."

Answer: Wise men and women receive counsel. According to Proverbs 14:12, "There is a way which seemeth right unto a man, but the end thereof are the ways of death." Matthew 7:13-14 gives direction on the best way: "Enter ye in at the strait gate: for wide is the gate, and broad is the way, that leadeth to destruction, and many there be which go in thereat: Because strait is the gate, and narrow is the way, which leadeth unto life, and few there be that find it."

Excuse: "I will take my chances."

Answer: God always has the last word. And if God is not the head of your life, you will not be saved. Why? Because if you take your chances, you don't have faith in God and His Word. When I read

His Word, this is what it tells me: "Trust in the LORD with all thine heart; and lean not unto thine own understanding" (Proverbs 3:5). So if you are taking your chances, you are out of the will of God.

As you can see, these excuses lead to destruction. Therefore, we must stop thinking we are more powerful than God, our Creator, and head the right way!

Chapter 4

What You Can Do

While you can do many things, I will give you a few ideas, and as you read His Word, you will see and know without a doubt what to do. Start by reading the Word of God daily. Also, get on your knees or stand up daily and pray. Your war room is where the battle is fought. Remember, we are at war with spiritual wickedness in high places. Those are places we can't see, so we have to pray in the spirit (in tongues) and let the Spirit (Holy Ghost) of the Lord fight for us. First

Corinthians 15:57 says, "But thanks be to God, which giveth us the victory through our Lord Jesus Christ." So give praise to our God daily!

Keeping What God Gives You

If you want to keep what God gives you, you need to walk in love as God tells us (2 Kings 4:8). When we stop loving one another, we begin to lose the power of God.

There is a season of rest, a time to refresh and continue to pray and give thanks, and we must know when that season is. (Read Matthew 18:1, 18; James 1:3.)

Celebrate Recovery

Many people have addictions and are working in darkness. To break through the darkness, we need Jesus. In man's eyes, it is not easy to overcome addiction, but we must put our trust in Jesus, trusting in His Word. What we do matters, and most of all, how we do it will define if we are being the salt and light God commanded us to be. (See Exodus 16:1-5.)

The Power of Yes

Second Corinthians 3:17 tells us, "Now the Lord is that Spirit: and where the Spirit of the Lord is, there is liberty."

The Word of God travels faster than human networking, and human networking can't override the Holy Ghost promotion (Matthew 8:8). Jeremiah 33:3 says, "Call unto me, and I will answer thee, and show thee great and mighty things, which thou knowest not." Furthermore, Jeremiah 29:11-12 tells us: "For I know the thoughts that I think toward you, saith the Lord, thoughts of peace, and not of evil, to give you an expected end. Then shall ye call upon me, and ye shall go and pray unto me, and I will hearken unto you." If God gives you instruction, He will not give you distractions. However, many people are so busy doing nothing, they can't see or understand the instruction.

If we have faith in and obedience to God, these things will push us into our blessings. "But without faith it is impossible to please him: for he that cometh to God must believe that he is, and that he is a rewarder of them that diligently seek him" (Hebrews 11:6).

Therefore, we must say yes to God and NO to the devil. After all, the Bible tells us, "Resist the devil, and he will flee from you" (James 4:7). Also, Daniel 11:32 says, "And such as do wickedly against the covenant shall he corrupt by flatteries: but the people that do know their God shall be strong, and do exploits."

When we are walking in God's grace, we are bold and fear no one because we know whose we are and that we have divine protection. (See Proverbs 28:1.)

In addition, we, as men and women of God, have the supernatural power of Samson. We just need to learn how to tap into it. Hopefully after reading this book, you will have a better understanding of who you are and your rights as a man or woman of God the Father. Read 2 Chronicles 16:9. We are in the bloodline of the lion of Judah. We have unspeakable power, but only if we are obedient to the Word of God.

We also have supernatural provision. God will provide for you so "fear not: believe only" (Luke 8:50). His Word says

He will never leave you or forsake you (Hebrews 13:5). On the other hand, says Joshua 24:20, "If ye forsake the Lord, and serve strange gods, then he will turn and do you hurt, and consume you, after that he hath done you good." Other "gods" may include cars, clothes, money, or other material things. In addition, Matthew 7:23 says, "And then will I profess unto them, I never knew you: depart from me, ye that work iniquity."

When we praise God, the result is increase and power, joy, and closeness to Him. Read these Bible verses about praising Him: Psalm 148, Ephesians 5:20, Hebrews 13:15, Psalm 67:5-6, Psalm 47:1, Psalm 100, Psalm 98:4, Psalm 95:1, Psalm 66:1-4, Isaiah 61, Psalm 40:2, 1 Peter 2:9, Psalm 5:11, Ephesians 5:18-20, Ephesians 5:4, Numbers 14:21, Psalm 50, James 1:5, and 1 Timothy 6:12.

Because every day is a contest and the devil is always trying to strip us of our blessings, we need to be on our guard always. Far from Jesus, doubt is the enemy of faith, is unhealthy, and is a sign of weakness. On the other hand, faith is a show of trust and strength, which brings us close to Jesus.

Matthew 14:27-31 provides a great example of faith; when you read it, fill in the blanks:

But straightway Jesus spake unto them, saying, Be of good cheer; it is I; be not afraid. And Peter answered him and said, Lord, if it be thou, bid me come unto thee on the water. And he said, Come. And when Peter was come down out of the ship, he walked on the water, to go to Jesus. But when he

What Have We Become?

saw the wind boisterous, he was _afraid_; and beginning to sink, he cried, saying, Lord, save me. [Who does this sound like?] And immediately Jesus stretched forth his hand, and caught him, and said unto him, O thou of _little faith_, wherefore didst thou _believe_?

When you stop acting on and trusting the Word of God, doubt will begin to set in. And doubt will take away God's best for you.

This is further expressed in Mark 6:5-6 (fill in the blanks): "And he could there do no mighty work, save that he laid his hands upon a few sick folk, and healed them. And he marvelled because of their ~~faith~~ _unbelief_. And he went round about the villages, teaching."

So if you are fighting for your life, be around people of faith. Do not hang around people of doubt.

To see the power of faith, read Mark 11:23.

Because people in the world today have no self-control and no standard, we need to put on the armor of God (Ephesians 6:10-17). When you put on the armor of God, you are putting on His Son Jesus. In the following passage, I want you to insert "Jesus" in the blanks and then read it again and again so you know who will fight your battles if you let Him. Verses 14-17 read: "Stand therefore, having your loins girt about with ___Jesus___, and having on the breastplate of ___Jesus___; and your feet shod with the preparation of the gospel of ___Jesus___; Above all, taking the shield of ___Jesus___, wherewith ye shall be able to quench all the fiery darts of the wicked. And take the helmet of ___Jesus___, and the sword of the Spirit, which is the word of God."

As Habakkuk 2:2 says, "Write the vision, and make it plain upon tables." If you don't have a vision, you need to get one and make it plain so you can stay on course, as I believe a man without a vision is going nowhere. In Hebrews 10:35, the Bible tells us if we don't have a vision, we need to get one: "Cast not away therefore your confidence, which hath great recompence of reward."

If we don't all have goals, we should. <u>Goals give us a purpose</u>; we keep pushing until we have accomplished our mission or met our goal. But for this to happen, we must do what His Word says: "For ye have need of patience, that, after ye have done the will of God, ye might receive the promise" (Hebrews 10:36). When we are obedient to God's Word, He rewards us; He will give us the desires of our heart. We need to follow His guideline for righteous living and not the way of the world, especially the way it is going today. If you really want to keep what God has given to you, stay on His team, follow His game plan, and become a sure winner. Everybody loves a winner. Stop the negative speaking, and start being positive in everything you do and say. Call those things that are not as though they were.

The Antichrist wants you to see only what will make you think what people in the world are doing is right. However, I want to tell you there is a greater system than the system of the Antichrist (1 John 4). That system is the powerful system of the Holy Spirit. The media is giving way to the cunningness and craftiness of the devil. While he doesn't have any power, he plays on people's weaknesses, and now people are weak because they refuse to stand up and be bold about the Word of God. The Word tells us, <u>ALL power belongs to God</u> (Psalm 62:11). The only power the devil has is what we give to him. Right now, we need to take back what we have given to him. You may be thinking, *How do I do that?* Start by putting God first in all that you do. Read His Word, pray, give thanks, praise Him, and fellowship with like-minded Christians, believers.

We have to put away all other gods that we put ahead of the real living God. As I mentioned earlier in this chapter, those other gods include money and other material possessions—basically anything you put ahead of God that becomes whom or what you worship more than the living God. If you keep your mind on God, you

What You Can Do

will be able to keep what He gives you. Here are the top five things for which I believe people pray to God, in no particular order:

- Money (to pay bills, and buy food and other things).
- Healing (to cure all types of diseases and illnesses).
- A new car.
- A new house.
- Relationships (to mend broken hearts and marriages).

This order may be different in your household, but the bottom line is these things are in your prayers.

There is nothing wrong with asking God for these things or having them. God sees and knows how you will use what He gives. However, when we receive something from God, I believe He wants us to be kind and generous to others by sharing. In our prayers, we should also pray for others and not be selfish and just think of ourselves all the time.

Given that, we ought to pray for:

- Family.
- Friends.
- Missionaries.
- Your pastor and his family.
- Ministers and their families.
- Church leaders.
- Our president.
- Our judicial system.
- Congress.
- World leaders.

There is so much we can pray for and be thankful for, and now we need prayer more than ever to break the back of the devil, who has a hold on some of our leaders. We can keep what we have been given; we just need to stay the course and follow the instruction book.

However, people are in the personal mode and not in the spirit. When you are in the personal mode, you are blocking the Spirit from moving in your life. (Read 2 Corinthians 6:16.) Let us use divine healing as an example. It comes through your human spirit. God only heals through FAITH, and it must come from the HEART. You may ask, "Why the heart?" This is where everything begins. (Read Proverbs 4:23 and Psalm 44:21.) Remember this: The closer you get to Jesus, the stronger your faith, and the further away you are from Jesus, the more doubtful you are of His Word. So, my friend, please get closer to Him. When you get closer to Him, you will feel His Spirit, which gives you these nine things:

- Affection of others (love).
- Exuberance about life (joy).
- Serenity (peace).
- A willingness to stick with things (patience).
- Compassion (kindness).
- Basic holiness (goodness).
- Loyalty (faithfulness).
- Not needing to force our energies (gentleness).
- Marshalling and directing our energies wisely (self-control).

Also remember, your labor in the Lord determines your reward, and the Lord rewards those who diligently seek Him (Hebrews 11:6).

Chapter 5

Prayer, Praise, and Thanksgiving

If we are not people of prayer, we should be. While most of us pray when we feel like praying, some of us don't pray at all, but expect God to answer our prayers. Especially if things are going great, we don't even pray or give thanks. But as soon as something undesirable happens in our lives, we get on our knees and beg God for help. Let me give you an example of what that looks and sounds like. Say you go to Wells Fargo bank, where you have an account with a zero balance because you have not deposited anything there in the past five months. You request to withdraw funds, but there is no money in the account. Guess what? You are not going to get anything out of the account because you did not put anything in.

That is what happens when you don't pray daily or only pray when you need God's help; God said we should always pray.

Luke 21:36 says, "Watch ye therefore, and pray always, that ye may be accounted worthy to escape all these things that shall come to pass, and to stand before the Son of man." And Luke 18:1 states, "And he spake a parable unto them to this end, that men ought always to pray, and not to faint." This means we should not fall away or give up. You see, we are to always make deposits in our accounts, for when we need to make withdrawals, we have sufficient prayers from which to withdraw. Our God is a God of prayer, and He wants us to call upon Him. We are His children, and we should be children of prayer.

The number one model prayer is the Lord's Prayer. The model prayer of the Lord is cherished by all Christians because of its simplicity, beautiful imagery, and instructive value. Jesus emphasized that we should pray with faith and simplicity (Matthew 6:7-8). Jesus drew great strength from His heavenly Father through prayer, and it was only natural for Him to teach His followers about the significance and meaning of prayer. Matthew's account of the Lord's Prayer (Matthew 6:9-13) comes from a portion of Jesus' Sermon on the Mount that warned against hypocrisy in prayer. Luke's version of the prayer consists of Jesus' response to a request from the disciples to "teach us to pray" (Luke 11:1). If you are a follower of Christ, this is your model for prayer.

I will try and break down the model prayer for you, and pray you will have a better understanding of what you are praying. The invocation of the prayer, "Our Father which art in heaven, hallowed be thy name" (Matthew 6:9), indicates the spirit of adoration and reverence in which the heavenly Father should be approached by His children.

Verse 10, "Thy kingdom come, Thy will be done in earth, as it is in heaven," expresses the longing for a society on earth where God's will is as perfectly done as it is in heaven. In our prayers, we should indicate our submission to the dominion and authority of God in our lives.

Then, verse 11, "Give us this day our daily bread," addresses a loving Father who is concerned for our physical welfare, and it expresses our dependence on Him for our physical needs.

Continuing, verse 12, "And forgive us our debts, as we forgive our debtors," is a petition for pardon as we approach God in a spirit of forgiveness toward others.

Next, verse 13 starts, "And lead us not into temptation, but deliver us from evil" and is a request for continual protection from the snares of Satan and all evil forces.

Finally, the closing of the prayer gives glory to God: "For thine is the kingdom, and the power, and the glory, for ever" (6:13). It appropriately attributes all power and glory to God for all eternity.

As you can see, prayer is not to be taken lightly. God wants us to pray. He wants us to communicate with Him daily. But as I said before, prayer is just one side of a two-winged bird, meaning we need something else to balance things out. Yes, God wants us to have balance in life in everything we do. If you have your spiritual life in order, I believe everything else will fall into place. This reminds me of what Matthew 6:33 says: "But seek ye first the kingdom of God, and his righteousness; and all these things shall be added unto you."

God has set a system in place, and if you follow it, you will not fail. It is when we try to reinvent what God has done that we begin to have problems. In Ephesians 4:14, the Bible tells us, "That we henceforth be no more children, tossed to and fro, and carried about with every wind of doctrine, by the sleight of men, and cunning craftiness, whereby they lie in wait to deceive."

When you look around at what is happening in today's world, you can get confused because of all the things coming at you all at once. You are having doubts about whom to believe or what to do. Now is the time for you to get in your war room and begin to pray, repenting and asking God to take control of your life. You must have a pure heart of faith when you pray. Remember, what God touches, He changes, so continue to pray for yourself, family, friends, other people, and our leaders. Pray for them in spite of how you think they are living. Simply, your job is to pray and let God handle the rest, the outcome. Last, I want you to really read this Scripture, meditate on it, and get in the battle because we need prayer warriors:

"If my people, which are called by my name, shall humble themselves, and pray, and seek my face, and turn from their wicked ways; then will I hear from heaven, and will forgive their sin, and will heal their land" (2 Chronicles 7:14). Now read verse 15: "Now mine eyes shall be open, and mine ears attent unto the prayer that is made in this place."

He is waiting on you to start praying, so humble yourselves, and get in the trenches and begin to send those prayers up to heaven. People, this is real; this is not a joke! Prayer can heal the sick! Prayer can save the lost! Prayer can mend the brokenhearted! Prayer can move all the mountains in your life! Just have faith and believe. He will see you through!

Next I will talk about the other wing of the bird, praise with thanksgiving.

We must give God praise and thanks every day, not just when things are going well. Praise Him in the morning and in the evening. As we say, when the praises go up, the blessings come down. So give thanks in both good and bad times. I believe God does inhabit the praises of His people. You may be wondering why I am saying this. When I read 1 Peter 2:9, it tells me we are "a chosen generation, a royal priesthood, an holy nation, a peculiar people; that [we] should shew forth the praises of him who hath called [us] out of darkness into his marvellous light." Yes, when we praise Him, He hears us! We owe Him our praise, and I don't think we praise Him enough for what He has done for us.

Worship encompasses feeling and deed; there are many expressions of it. Worship includes praise and thanksgiving, which may be expressed privately or publicly, and is a choice the person praising makes. I believe the single most important act of worship for Christians is the unqualified presentation of themselves to God as obedient servants. The dedication involves the body and the mind. The body contains the tools by which the will of God is carried out. The mind coordinates the action that the body will execute. When these are devoted to God, they become instruments He can use to affect His will on earth. Such faithful and joyous action makes one's life a performance of worship.

Psalm 50:23 says, "Whoso offereth praise glorifieth me: and to him that ordereth his conversation aright will I shew the salvation of God." Brothers and sisters, you now see why it is so important to have balance in your spiritual life. When we are complete in Him, we are stronger, smarter, and wiser, and we walk with the power of the Holy Spirit every day.

Further, the importance and spiritual benefits of thanksgiving in our prayer life cannot be emphasized enough. The Bible tells us God resists the proud, but gives grace to the humble (James 4:6). The question is, how do you become humble? You become humble by being thankful. A good rule is to "be careful [worried] for nothing" (Philippians 4:6), be prayerful in all things (1 Thessalonians 5:18), and be thankful for anything. The main thing we are to thank God for is His work in our creation, which we are reminded in Psalm 100. Also, one of the most powerful songs we can sing comes from Revelation 4:11, and this is what it says: "Thou art worthy, O Lord, to receive glory and honour and power: for thou hast created all things, and for thy pleasure they are and were created."

I pray that you have asked God to open the eyes of your understanding, that you may know His Word. Here are two verses I would like for you to remember:

Proverbs 4:7: "Wisdom is the principal thing; therefore get wisdom: and with all thy getting get understanding."

Proverbs 9:9: "Give instruction to a wise man, and he will be yet wiser: teach a just man, and he will increase in learning."

To have that balance in our spiritual life, following are a few things I believe we need, in no particular order.

- Faith—with faith comes hope.
- Trust—with trust comes belief.
- Prayer—with prayer comes answers.

- Praise—with praise comes blessing.
- Thanksgiving—with thanksgiving comes a spirit of appreciation.
- If you don't like the game you are in, seek my Lord and Savior, Jesus Christ. He is a game-changer.

When we praise the Lord, He blesses us. I believe praise brings increase into our lives. Read Psalm 107:31. We all want our children to be blessed and highly favored; I know I want my family to receive every benefit God has. I truly believe those benefits will come through obedience, and that means we must give Him praise.

Note: You can't be a complainer and praise God. People of faith don't complain; they praise and give thanks. Therefore, we really need to be people of praise.

When this happens, you will see God move like you've never seen before. So start praising and thanking Him now—not tomorrow. Take a few seconds now and say the following five things five times. I know it may sound strange, but it brings joy and a smile to God to see His people praising Him.

- Bless the Lord.
- Thank You, Jesus.
- Praise the Lord.
- Glory to God.
- Hallelujah.

Say these things daily from the heart; mean what you are saying. Remember, you can't fool God; what you say must be pure and from the heart.

When you form a habit, it will come naturally. This is what God wants from

Prayer, Praise, and Thanksgiving

us, to praise Him naturally, when things are *good or bad*. Only you and God know when and how you praise Him. This is how it should be because it is a personal thing between you and God. People will see the benefits of your praises and worship from the blessing of the Lord. There is power in praise!

Remember, God gives us the power to choose. Your identity is in Christ. Your habits are what you choose, and your hang-ups and pride do not make you. The world wants you to conform to its way of life, living in darkness, watering down the salt we are to be spreading, keeping our light in hiding (Romans 1:21, James 4:4-8).

To help you get where you need to be, focus on the following seven things.

- Focus on God's power and not your own.

- Focus on good, not bad, things.
- Focus on walking by faith in what God says.
- Focus on who is helping you.
- Focus on praising and worshiping Him.
- Focus on praying and giving thanks.
- Focus on love and not hate.

If you keep your focus on these things, you will be on your way to receiving the benefits and blessings of God.

Chapter 6

The End-Time Is Near—Are You Spiritually Ready?

As the end-time is near, you need to think about whether you are spiritually ready. You may be thinking, *Why is he talking about the end-time, and what does this have to do with what is going on in the world today?* I am glad you are asking these questions because if you don't, you will never know how to prepare for what is about to happen. The Bible spells out everything you need to know. All we have to do is read the *basic instructions before leaving earth* (BIBLE), and apply it to our lives, not following man's laws when they go against the Word of God. If you go against the Creator, eternal damnation will be the result. I will quote a few Scriptures and give you others to read in hopes that you will ask God to open your eyes to see what He has told us to do. Please do not let your oil run out because we do not know the day or hour when the Bridegroom will return. Keep plenty of oil in your lamp, and you will not have to go out to get more and miss the return of the Bridegroom.

Please read the story of the ten virgins (Matthew 25:1-14). You will get a full understanding of what I am talking about regarding the oil and being ready for the return of our Lord and Savior, Jesus Christ.

To learn more about His return, read Matthew 24:

And Jesus went out, and departed from the temple: and his disciples came to him for to shew him the buildings of the temple. And Jesus said unto them, See ye not all these things? Verily I say unto you, There shall not be left here one stone upon another, that shall not be thrown down.

And as he sat upon the mount of Olives, the disciples came unto him privately, saying, Tell us, when shall these things be? and what shall be the sign of thy coming, and of the end of the world?

And Jesus answered and said unto them, Take heed that no man deceive you. For many shall come in my name, saying, I am Christ; and shall deceive many. And ye shall hear of wars and rumours of wars: see that ye be not troubled: for all these things must come to pass, but the end is not yet. For nation shall rise against nation, and kingdom against kingdom: and there shall be famines, and pestilences, and earthquakes, in divers places. All these are the beginning of sorrows.

Then shall they deliver you up to be afflicted, and shall kill you: and ye shall be hated of all nations for my name's sake. And then shall many be offended, and shall betray one another, and shall hate one another. And many false prophets shall rise, and shall deceive many. And because iniquity shall abound, the love of many shall wax cold.

But he that shall endure unto the end, the same shall be saved. And this gospel of the kingdom shall be preached in all the world for a witness unto all nations; and then shall the end come.

When ye therefore shall see the abomination of desolation, spoken of by Daniel the prophet, stand in the holy place, (whoso readeth, let him understand:) Then let them which be in Judaea flee into the mountains: Let him which is on the housetop not come down to take any thing out of his house: Neither let him which is in the field return back to take his clothes. And woe unto them that are with child, and to them that give suck in those days! But pray ye that your flight be not in the winter, neither on the sabbath day: For then shall be great tribulation, such as was not since the beginning of the world to this time, no, nor ever shall be.

And except those days should be shortened, there should no flesh be saved: but for the elect's sake those days shall be shortened. Then if any man shall say unto you, Lo, here is Christ, or there; believe it not. For there shall arise false Christs, and false prophets, and shall shew great signs and wonders; insomuch that, if it were possible, they shall deceive the very elect. Behold, I have told you before.

Wherefore if they shall say unto you, Behold, he is in the desert; go not forth: behold, he is in the secret chambers; believe it not. For as the lightning cometh out of the east, and shineth even unto the west; so shall also the coming of the Son of man be. For wheresoever the carcase is, there will the eagles be gathered together.

Immediately after the tribulation of those days shall the sun be darkened, and the moon shall not give her light, and the stars shall fall from heaven, and the powers of the heavens shall be shaken:

And then shall appear the sign of the Son of man in heaven: and then shall all the tribes of the earth mourn, and they shall see the Son of man coming in the clouds of heaven with power and great glory. And he shall send his angels with a great sound of a trumpet, and they shall gather together his elect from the four winds, from one end of heaven to the other.

Now learn a parable of the fig tree; When his branch is yet tender, and putteth forth leaves, ye know that summer is nigh: So likewise ye, when ye shall see all these things, know that it is near, even at the doors. Verily I say unto you, This generation shall not pass, till all these things be fulfilled. Heaven and earth shall pass away, but my words shall not pass away.

But of that day and hour knoweth no man, no, not the angels of heaven, but my Father only. But as the days of Noah were, so shall also the coming of the Son of man be. For as in the days that were before the flood they were eating and drinking, marrying and giving in marriage, until the day that Noe entered into the ark, and knew not until the flood came, and took them all away; so shall also the coming of the Son of man be. Then shall two be in the field; the one shall be taken, and the other left. Two women shall be grinding at the mill; the one shall be taken, and the other left.

Watch therefore: for ye know not what hour your Lord doth come. But know this, that if the goodman of the house had known in what watch the thief would come, he would have watched, and would not have suffered his house to be broken up. Therefore be ye also ready: for in such an hour as ye think not the Son of man cometh.

Who then is a faithful and wise servant, whom his lord hath made ruler over his household, to give them meat in due season? Blessed is that servant, whom his lord when he cometh shall find so doing. Verily I say unto you, That he shall make him ruler over all his goods. But and if that evil servant shall say in his heart, My lord delayeth his coming; and shall begin to smite his fellowservants, and to eat and drink with the drunken; The lord of that servant shall come in a day when he looketh not for him, and in an hour that he is not aware of, and shall cut him asunder, and appoint him his portion with the hypocrites: there shall be weeping and gnashing of teeth.

It is amazing how a book that was written more than two thousand years ago can be on point today. If you want to know what is going to happen, read the Bible—it will lay it out for you. If you don't believe God exists after reading the Bible, you have the problem of denial. Everything is being played out before your eyes every day. I would tell you that Satan has blinded your minds and eyes, just like he did mine twenty years ago. But I had a praying grandmother, and I married a praying woman, who keeps praying for me. Now that I am on the other side, I, along with my Christian brothers and sisters around the world, will be praying for you and your family. We want you to let go and let God work in you.

To give you a little more knowledge of what the Word of God says, I'll take the liberty of stating 2 Timothy 3:1-17:

> This know also, that in the last days perilous times shall come. [These are the times we are in today.] For men shall be lovers of their own selves, covetous, boasters, proud, blasphemers, disobedient to parents, unthankful, unholy, without natural affection, trucebreakers, false accusers, incontinent, fierce, despisers of those that are good, traitors, heady, highminded, lovers of pleasures more than lovers of God; Having a form of godliness, but denying the power thereof: from such turn away.

For of this sort are they which creep into houses, and lead captive silly women laden with sins, led away with divers lusts, ever learning, and never able to come to the knowledge of the truth. Now as Jannes and Jambres withstood Moses, so do these also resist the truth: men of corrupt minds, reprobate concerning the faith. But they shall proceed no further: for their folly shall be manifest unto all men, as theirs also was.

But thou hast fully known my doctrine, manner of life, purpose, faith, longsuffering, charity, patience, persecutions, afflictions, which came unto me at Antioch, at Iconium, at Lystra; what persecutions I endured: but out of them all the Lord delivered me. Yea, and all that will live godly in Christ Jesus shall suffer persecution. But evil men and seducers shall wax worse and worse, deceiving, and being deceived. But continue thou in the things which thou hast learned and hast been assured of, knowing of whom thou hast learned them; And that from a child thou hast known the holy scriptures, which are able to make thee wise unto salvation through faith which is in Christ Jesus. All scripture is given by inspiration of God, and is profitable for doctrine, for reproof, for correction, for instruction in righteousness: That the man of God may be perfect, thoroughly furnished unto all good works.

Here are a few more Scriptures you should study:

- 1 Corinthians 15.
- Romans 8:22-23.
- 1 Thessalonians 2:13.
- Luke 21:36.

Looking around the world today, it's apparent we are not ready, and if we don't do something about it, we will be caught without oil in our lamps. When this happens, we will be in trouble, so why wait for that to happen when we can get ready now and enjoy the benefits God has provided for us?

The Antichrist is already here. He has his nonbeliever at work in the judicial system and political arena in all cities and states. They are being bold in letting people know where they stand—and they are not believers of Christ; they are not living according to the Word of God. The prince of this world—Satan—has blinded them to understanding the Word of God.

As men and women of God, who believe in the Father, Son, and Holy Spirit, we must let them know that. We must be bold in speaking the Word of God; we can't be wimps, relinquishing our power to the devil. Please understand, the only power the devil has is that which we give him. He draws his power from your weaknesses and lack of a prayer life. With the end-time near, we need prayer more than ever. Why? Prayer opens the door to God's power. We also must begin to praise Him more and more each day. Why must we do that? I believe praise closes down the devil's operation. I believe we, as a body, have grown weak in these areas, along with not being bold. We have become weak concerning the things of God. Though we have the victory in Christ Jesus, we are being bullied by the devil, causing fear to set in. This is why we are in the times of Sodom and Gomorrah.

Because it is something we must do and, in fact, are commanded to do, allow me to speak a little more about praise and worship. I believe God inhabits the praise of His people. Now I will tell you a Bible story of two men of God. Their names were Paul and Silas, and they were disciples of Christ, preaching and teaching the Word of God. They were told to stop preaching, but they did not because they feared God and not man. They were thrown into prison, but they dialed in to the hot line straight to the King of Kings. You may be wondering how they did that. I am glad you have your thinking cap on. They began to pray and sing praises unto

God, and the prisoners heard them. Then, as Acts 16:26 tells us, "suddenly there was a great earthquake, so that the foundations of the prison were shaken: and immediately all the doors were opened, and every one's bands were loosed."

I encourage you to read the rest of the story, in Acts 16, for yourself. The moral of this story is through prayer and praise, the doors of heaven released God's power to His people.

We too need to get bold in the Word of God! We need to be like Paul and Silas daily in our prayers, praise, and thanksgiving. Remember 2 Timothy 1:7: "For God hath not given us the spirit of fear; but of POWER, and of LOVE, and of a SOUND MIND" (emphasis added). So the question is, why are you so afraid of man? Unleash the power you have to make things right, to spread the gospel, to help others who are in need of mentoring.

The Seed: Our Children

As we near the end-time, the main focus of the devil is our children. Look around, and see what is happening with our seeds. We need to get this situation under control—that is, get back to the basics, as stated in the book of Deuteronomy chapter 6. As you read the chapter, pay close attention to verse 7: "And thou shalt teach them diligently unto thy children, and shalt talk of them when thou sittest in thine house, and when thou walkest by the way, and when thou liest down, and when thou risest up." If this is not being done, your child is at great risk of being caught in the devil's net. Not only is the seed being affected by the devil in the United States, but all over the world. Children are being misused and abused, and it needs to stop. We need to show them how to be bold in the Word of God, be strong and not weak.

God has entrusted you to take care of your children, not for them to grow up and dictate to you how things are going to be. We must start teaching them before they can walk or talk. Since kids will emulate what they see you do, start setting a godly example in the way you talk and act. Show them how you pray to, praise, and give thanks to God. Never give up on your children because God has not given up on you. And He will never give up on you, so let us protect our little ones from the tactics of the devil. Remember, he has many ways, but the Holy Spirit knows them all. So brothers and sisters, let all of us repent and be saved, for the end-time is near.

Recently when I was on my computer, *The View* was on TV, and the hostesses were talking about a lady who refused to issue marriage licenses to gay couples. I thought how we watch shows daily featuring people who are not Christian and do not believe in the Word of God. Our children are hearing what they are saying, and believing them. We must stop looking and listening, and then we can stop our children from doing so. Show hostesses also said they support a high school boy who started wearing a dress and heels, let his hair grow long, and wanted to start using the girls locker room. This is an example of what is happening to our children—the words of non-Christians, non-believers of God are filling the minds of our children with the sinful evil of the devil. We must stand up and be bold about God's Word. We must hide the Word in our hearts so we can quote it to people in hopes that they may see what they are doing to children. People must know they can't change the Word of God—if you were born male, you are a male, and if you were born female, you are a female. God does not make mistakes; it is man that allows the devil to implant these feelings in us that are against the will of God. Trust me, someone will pay for what is happening; keep in mind Sodom and Gomorrah. Time is running out. With one accord, we need to act now. We need to *pray until something happens* (PUSH).

Chapter 7

The Promises of God

If we are obedient to God's Word, we will see several of His promises, and we will see our lives change. All God's promises come with conditions—if you do this, you will receive that; if you do that, you will receive this. Following are several of the promises God has made to us. When you read them, know this is how the world system is set up. If you want to know about this world, go to the One who created it. Here are several of His great promises:

Salvation

"Verily, verily, I say unto you, He that heareth my word, and believeth on him that sent me, hath everlasting life, and shall not come into condemnation; but is passed from death unto life" (John 5:24).

"I am the door: by me if any man enter in, he shall be saved, and shall go in and out, and find pasture" (John 10:9).

"I am come a light into the world, that whosoever believeth on me should not abide in darkness" (John 12:46).

"That if thou shalt confess with thy mouth the Lord Jesus, and shalt believe in thine heart that God hath raised him from the dead, thou shalt be saved. For with the heart man believeth unto righteousness;

and with the mouth confession is made unto salvation" (Romans 10:9-10).

God's Rewards

"He that receiveth a prophet in the name of a prophet shall receive a prophet's reward; and he that receiveth a righteous man in the name of a righteous man shall receive a righteous man's reward" (Matthew 10:41).

"But when thou doest alms, let not thy left hand know what thy right hand doeth: That thine alms may be in secret: and thy Father which seeth in secret himself shall reward thee openly" (Matthew 6:3-4).

"Cast not away therefore your confidence, which hath great recompence of reward. For ye have need of patience, that, after ye have done the will of God, ye might receive the promise" (Hebrews 10:35-36).

"And he said unto me, It is done. I am Alpha and Omega, the beginning and the end. I will give unto him that is athirst of the fountain of the water of life freely. He that overcometh shall inherit all things; and I will be his God, and he shall be my son" (Revelation 21:6-7).

"And whatsoever ye do, do it heartily, as to the Lord, and not unto men; knowing that of the Lord ye shall receive the reward of the inheritance: for ye serve the Lord Christ" (Colossians 3:23-24).

Success

"Commit thy works unto the LORD, and thy thoughts shall be established" (Proverbs

16:3). "When a man's ways please the Lord, he maketh even his enemies to be at peace with him" (Proverbs 16:7).

"Delight thyself also in the Lord: and he shall give thee the desires of thine heart. Commit thy way unto the Lord; trust also in him; and he shall bring it to pass" (Psalm 37:4-5).

"Blessed is the man that walketh not in the counsel of the ungodly, nor standeth in the way of sinners, nor sitteth in the seat of the scornful. But his delight is in the law of the Lord; and in his law doth he meditate day and night. And he shall be like a tree planted by the rivers of water, that bringeth forth his fruit in his season; his leaf also shall not wither; and whatsoever he doeth shall prosper" (Psalm 1:1-3).

Faith

"And Jesus said unto them, Because of your unbelief: for verily I say unto you, If ye have faith as a grain of mustard seed, ye shall say unto this mountain, Remove hence to yonder place; and it shall remove; and nothing shall be impossible unto you. Howbeit this kind goeth not out but by prayer and fasting" (Matthew 17:20-21).

"But without faith it is impossible to please him: for he that cometh to God must believe that he is, and that he is a rewarder of them that diligently seek him" (Hebrews 11:6).

"Even so faith, if it hath not works, is dead, being alone."

"And when the disciples saw it, they marvelled, saying, How soon is the fig tree withered away! Jesus answered and said unto them, Verily I say unto you, If ye have faith, and doubt not, ye shall not only do this which is done to the fig tree, but also if ye shall say unto this mountain, Be thou removed, and be thou cast into the sea; it shall be done. And all things, whatsoever ye shall ask in prayer, believing, ye shall receive" (Matthew 21:20-22).

The Holy Spirit

"And, behold, I send the promise of my Father upon you: but tarry ye in the city of Jerusalem, until ye be endued with power from on high" (Luke 24:49).

"Verily, verily, I say unto you, He that believeth on me, the works that I do shall he do also; and greater works than these shall he do; because I go unto my Father. And whatsoever ye shall ask in my name, that will I do, that the Father may be glorified in the Son. If ye shall ask any thing in my name, I will do it. If ye love me, keep my commandments. And I will pray the Father, and he shall give you another Comforter, that he may abide with you for ever; Even the Spirit of truth; whom the world cannot receive, because it seeth him not, neither knoweth him: but ye know him; for he dwelleth with you, and shall be in you. I will not leave you comfortless: I will come to you" (John 14:12-18).

"But ye shall receive power, after that the Holy Ghost is come upon you: and ye shall be witnesses unto me both in Jerusalem, and in all Judaea, and in Samaria, and unto the uttermost part of the earth" (Acts 1:8).

Healing

"Is any sick among you? Let him call for the elders of the church; and let them pray over him, anointing him with oil in the name of the Lord: And the prayer of faith shall save the sick, and the Lord shall raise him up; and if he have committed sins, they shall be forgiven him" (James 5:14-15).

"Bless the LORD, O my soul: and all that is within me, bless his holy name. Bless the LORD, O my soul, and forget not all his benefits: Who forgiveth all thine iniquities; who healeth all thy diseases" (Psalm 103:1-3).

"But he was wounded for our transgressions, he was bruised for our iniquities: the chastisement of our peace was upon him; and with his stripes we are healed" (Isaiah 53:5).

"Who his own self bare our sins in his own body on the tree, that we, being dead to sins, should live unto righteousness: by whose stripes ye were healed" (1 Peter 2:24).

Forgiveness

"For if ye forgive men their trespasses, your heavenly Father will also forgive you: But if ye forgive not men their trespasses, neither will your Father forgive your trespasses" (Matthew 6:14-15).

"In whom we have redemption through his blood, the forgiveness of sins, according to the riches of his grace" (Ephesians 1:7).

"If we confess our sins, he is faithful and just to forgive us our sins, and to cleanse us from all unrighteousness" (1 John 1:9).

"Be it known unto you therefore, men and brethren, that through this man is preached unto you the forgiveness of sins: and by him all that believe are justified from all things, from which ye could not be justified by the law of Moses" (Acts 13:38).

During my study, I came across a number of additional promises God has for us. Unfortunately, we are missing out on so much. We let too many distractions keep us from the Word of God, and we lose out on all the benefits He has promised us. As I said before, all of God's promises have conditions, I believe the system was set up this way so everyone would be on the same level when they start. Let's take a look at a few things to which you may be able to relate.

The first is work. If you have a job, you must work before you get paid. Then you have access to all the benefits money can buy. Let's look at school. To move on to the next grade, you must pass tests. If you want to graduate, you must have enough units or credits. My point is, there are conditions for everything we do in life, and the Word of God is the cornerstone of the system in which we live. We are saved by grace and not by anything we have done. That grace comes through obedience; we can enjoy all the benefits God has given to us if we are obedient to His Word. ("If ye be willing and obedient, ye shall eat the good of the land," Isaiah 1:19.)

There is power in obedience, but we have lost that power because we are letting the devil suck it out of us. "How are

The Promises of God

we getting weak?" you ask. I am glad you asked. As I stated before, we are following the way of the world and going against the Word of God by allowing man to change the principles of God. If we don't change the directions in which we are going, we will not have any oil in our lamps when the Bridegroom returns. And trust the Word of God—the end-time is very near.

To change direction, here are some things you can start doing:

- Pray night and day.
- Sing praises to the Lord daily.
- Read His Word daily.
- Give thanks daily.
- Forgive others.
- Have faith, trust, and believe God's Word.
- Show love toward others.
- Help others who are in need.

- Spread the gospel to the world.
- Teach your children (the seed).

During my study, I created a Promise Circle (to follow). I came up with twenty-two promises that God has for us, covering everything we would need in this life on earth.

For us to enjoy all of this, we must have one thing. Fill in the blank oval with that one word from this list that will bring them together:

- Love.
- Faith.
- Trust.
- Belief.
- Obedience.
- Hope.

The one word that belongs in the center is "_____"

When we have this, we can enjoy all the promises of God.

A Testimony That Your Prayers Are Being Heard

I was working at Luke AFB as the fitness center director in Glendale, Arizona. In April 2013, the government started downsizing, and positions were being cut. One morning, my supervisor came to my office and said my position had been cut and they had until August 23 to place me in another job. Well, that did not sit well with my spirit, so I got on the phone and started calling my counterparts around the Air Force who had the same job title I had. I asked each one if their job was cut, and each said no. Then, I became concerned about why mine was the only position in the Air Force that was cut when it was supposedly an Air Force-wide cut. When I called the headquarters to find out, to my surprise, it was not the Air Force that cut my position. It was the operation officer and the commander, both of whom had resigned by the time all of this had happened. So I went to the new commander, and he said he would try to fix the situation.

I told my wife, and we began praying to God about it. I told God I was not ready to leave the job I was doing and I wanted to leave on my terms. So I asked Him to let me keep my job until I was ready to leave. I began to thank Him every night and day for letting me keep my job.

A week before the 23rd, I received a call from the human resources office telling me they could not find me a job. I asked if they looked at other bases, and they said they did not have the money to do that. I spoke with Chief Smith, the sergeant major, who said he would make some calls. A week before the deadline, the commander called me into his office and said he had a position for me. After he told me what I would be doing, I told him I did not want that type of job. He said he would keep trying. I mentioned that we only had a week; time was running out. In the meantime, when people kept asking me when I would be leaving or if I had a job, I would always say, "I am not going anywhere."

I never gave up. I thanked God every day and night for my job. When August 22 came, no one called and said he had a job for me. Now, here is the kicker: If they could not find me a job, I would be out of a job. Yes, jobless. On the 23rd at

5 a.m., my cell phone rang. I was up getting ready to hit the gym for my workout. On the phone was Chief Smith, and he said: "Stoney, you are good to go. You will not be leaving. You still have your job at the fitness center." I said, "THANK YOU, JESUS! HALLELUJAH! PRAISE THE LORD!"

Indeed, the Lord hears our prayers! So keep praying and being obedient to His Word, and just see the benefits you reap.

CPSIA information can be obtained
at www.ICGtesting.com
Printed in the USA
LVOW01s0249230616
493727LV00005B/6/P